HOW TO GRADUATE COLLEGE DEBT-FREE

WITH

MONEY IN THE BANK

Shanice Miller

HOW TO GRADUATE COLLEGE DEBT-FREE

WITH

MONEY IN THE BANK

Shanice Miller

How to Graduate College Debt-Free WITH Money in the Bank™
Copyright © 2014 Shanice Miller

Shanice Miller also conducts workshops, seminars, and other events. For more information, visit www.debtfreecollegegrad.com

Printed in the United States

How to Graduate College Debt-Free WITH Money in the Bank™

Shanice Miller

ISBN: 978-1-49444-804-2

Table of Contents

Introduction

School did not prepare me for college. In fact, I do not think it really prepares anyone. No one told me about costs associated with going to college. Guidance counselors don't tell you anything about the cost of books or the cost of each class. They do not tell you the difference in private schools versus public schools.

They may suggest that you should apply for scholarships, but no one really stressed it. And just like any other person, I procrastinated with applying for scholarships. I didn't think it was that serious. I was only a freshman in high school after all, I figured it could wait. Plus, who really applies for scholarships their freshman year? Are there any scholarships even available for ninth graders to even apply to? At the time, I did not bother finding the answers to these questions that I had since college was so far away (at least I thought it was). Later, I discovered that there are in fact scholarships that high school freshman can apply for. There are even scholarships that elementary and middle school students are eligible to apply to! I could not believe that people were really thinking about scholarships that early on, but they are. It really is never too early to start scholarship searching. But, since I was a procrastinator…

Freshman year quickly turned to Sophomore year which quickly turned to Junior year which ended up being my Senior year in no time. I thought I had a lot of time, but in the blink of an eye, all of that time disappeared.

Now I was running short on time in my first month of my Senior year of high school and, to top things off, I was now worried that if I applied to scholarships, I most likely would not win them. There are millions of people applying to scholarships, right? What are the odds that I would be someone that the judges would select to win the scholarship money out of all the people that were applying? Only the super intelligent valedictorian of the class wins scholarships, right? Or even the top five students of each class are the ones to win the full-ride scholarships? I was nowhere close to being the valedictorian or even one of the top five students in my senior class and I was not a super star athlete either. They get all of the scholarship money too, don't they? Should I even bother with applying to scholarships if I have no chance of winning them?

I allowed these negative thoughts of doubt and worry to consume my mind to the point where I convinced myself to not even apply myself much for scholarships. I went online and applied to only one scholarship. When I did not hear anything back from that scholarship, I used that one solo experience as justification that "scholarships weren't for me" and did not bother to apply to any others for a while. In my mind, I had just proved to myself all of the thoughts that I had been thinking--- that I was not smart enough to win scholarships or athletic enough. Later I learned that you will not win every scholarship that you apply to. You have to choose scholarships that you are eligible for and that are specifically tailored for you and your likes. I also learned that the only way you can guarantee that you will NOT win the scholarship is if you do not apply.

Now, it was around my spring break and I only had a few months left in high school. The financial aid award letters had come in and I had to make some big decisions about where I would attend college. Some colleges gave me a little bit of money while others gave me a lot. Should I go with the school that my heart is set on or should I go with the school that is best for my wallet?

At another blink of an eye, I was a college freshman with no real clue what my major or career should be. I thought I did, but I was completely wrong.

Looking back on everything, I encountered a lot of confusion and frustration. All of which could have been avoided... with the right guidance. But that's just it! A lot of people, even guidance counselors, do not always have the right guidance or advice for you. Some guidance counselors are overworked and overwhelmed so they will not have the time to tell you what to do. While other guidance counselors that you may encounter do not know much about searching and applying for scholarships. And colleges are not going to tell you either because colleges are businesses... BIG businesses. They need to keep generating money--- YOUR MONEY--- to stay open.

Chapter 1

<u>Don't</u> Do This:

The Facts on College DEBT

"I have about $50,000 in college debt." –S. C. (Rockville, MD)

"I have $19,000 worth of debt just from my last 2 years of college." –Mindy Lee (Leesburg, VA)

"I graduated with $38,000 in debt" -Miah R. (Silver Spring, MD)

These three people and I have the same college profile. We are all women and attended the same dental school at the same time for the same program. However, they ended up with debt and I didn't. What was the difference? How did I graduate college debt free?

These three weren't the only ones that graduated with debt…

Many people all over the United States and other areas have graduated with student loan debt, which has affected them greatly. They have spoken out about it in an attempt to prevent others from making their same mistakes and to raise awareness on StudentLoanJustice.org. My warning to you, DON'T be like them.

One example, Helen from Kentucky states, "I attended the University of Kentucky. I earned an undergraduate degree in Social Work, and two graduate degrees---one in Social Work and the other in Education. Since I earned all these degrees, I thought that I would get a good paying job, and have a wonderful career. Needless to say, I owe student loans over $100,000 and I have a very low paying job making approximately $34,000 a year. I am so stressed out about this debt, because I don't even earn enough money to pay my mortgage. If I had any idea that attending school and earning a degree would cause this much hardship, I would have never gone! I tried everything to get these loans forgiven, however no such luck. I work with disadvantage youth in one of the poorest neighborhoods in Kentucky. The student loan people just keep adding interest to the $100,000. I don't see any way out, and I feel like I'm drowning in debt!"

Another example is Erica, who states, "I took numerous loans out for the California Culinary Academy from April 2003 to May 2004 and they were bought out by Sallie Mae. Interest rates were at the highest due to marginal credit history and I am not in the bracket to receive too much of Government aide. Right now I am in deferment because I owe approximately 1,100.00 a month when, as a chef, we make nowhere near that for the cost of living. I am also out of work due to my seasonal job (being of 3 seasons a year). Makes you wonder why you tried to better yourself in the first place."

Damian, from New York, is another victim of student loan debt and its negative impacts. He says, "I borrowed money for school. I believe the actual amount I was loaned totaled somewhere in the area of $30,000. Unfortunately, my loan went into default, and then into judgment. I am now paying interest only on the outrageous sum of $77,000. Interest and penalties have practically tripled the principal of the loans and are still accruing daily. I will probably be paying this off for the rest of my natural born life. This is the price of education in our fare country."

Chris Martin is from Colorado. His story is as follows. "I borrowed $34,000 total, but ended up owing $48,000 as of right now. I graduated with a 4 year degree in mid June 2006. My loan is due to start repayment in January. I have saved every penny I earn to pay towards this loan. I have only had the standard deferment all students have the option to have while attending full time in school. My payments begin at $634 per month. I did not expect that this loan would gain so much in fees in just a few short months since I graduated. I am sure it is legal, and that I simply should have read and understood in greater depth the terms of the promissory note and that of the repayment schedule is subject to change as explained to me recently by the loan counselor. I have yet to begin my first scheduled repayment and my loan is increasing my debt quickly!"

Then we have David who defaulted on loans to become a chiropractor and now is unable to renew his license due to defaulting on those loans. He went from owing $40,000 in 1989 to $320,000 in

2005 and states, "I can't renew my license to make a living, much less make payments on the loans and have experienced feelings of hopelessness, despair, no self-esteem, depression, suicide, etc., etc."

And Michael from Texas who didn't finish college due to not having enough money to finish but still had to repay the loans that he borrowed for his first few years.

We also have Lucia from Florida who borrowed $40,000 in 2004 with a monthly loan repayment plan of $829 a month. She now feels like "College is supposed to be the beginning of our lives, our future and after all of our hard work all we get is a huge amount of debt that most of us will probably drown in."

Fox News reported in the article, "Analysis New studies weigh college value and costs" that the total student debt in the US hit $1 trillion this year. (Yes, that's $1,000,000,000,000!) The article continues on to state that 40% of students left college with debt. The average amount of debt that a college student has is $22,000 and the average 4 year college with tuition plus room and board is over $17,000 just for one year. (These figures don't include other fees like living expenses, college textbooks, and travel expenses.) As you can see through other people's testimonials and this report that student loan debt is not a joke. It's a very serious matter that impacts people's lives for many years, sometimes even decades, after getting the initial loan amount.

Quite frankly, I can see how so many people get in trouble with student loan debt. Say you needed $10,000 for this semester to take classes. So you take out a loan, but that $10,000 loan only covers this one semester, your first semester, you still have 7 more semesters to go. So then you take out another $10,000 loan to get through your first year. Then another $10,000 and another $10,000 and another $10,000 all the way until you get to graduation.

You didn't tally up the total costs of those loans; all you did was sign a paper. Now, you are at graduation day with $80,000 worth of student loans, not including interest and fees. The amount of student loans that children sign up for does not seem tangible until after graduation because the money is not coming directly out of their pockets.

So you are probably wondering what can you and your child do to avoid some or all of this student loan debt?

DON'T GET STUDENT LOANS.

That was advice that my mom gave me. She did not have money to help towards my college education, but I wasn't supposed to take out any student loans either? How in the world was I supposed to get through all 4 years of college without student loans and with no money from her? At the time I was confused and challenged her statement. Little did I know she was on to something.

Chapter 2

The Blind Leading the Blind:

*How Listening to Misinformed People Can Cost
Your Child Thousands or More!*

When I first starting thinking about college, I thought that I wanted to be a graphic designer. I always enjoyed art and computers and I took a class and loved it. So when people would ask if I was going to college and what my plan was I would tell them I was going to college, not sure which one, but wanted to do graphic design. A co-worker told me that he went to Boston University, loved it, and they have a great art/ graphic design program. So I started thinking about Boston University as a potential college option and daydreaming about how great it would be.

I thought about the perfectly green lawn that I would sit on and study on a sunny day after walking with my friends from the library while other college students passed us on the sidewalk. Pretty much I thought about everything that the college's brochure portrayed. However, after I started researching the college I realized that it probably was not the college for me. See my co-worker told me how great of a college it was but failed to mention the expensive price of attending all four years. Here is a breakdown of the cost to attend:

Tuition	$42,400
Room (depending on type of accommodation)	$8,600
Board (most dining plans)	$4,590
Fees	$594
Total Billed Expenses	**$56,184**

These are the fees for 2012 from Boston University's website. This means that for each year, I would have to figure out how to come up with at least $56,184 not including my own living expenses. For all 4 years there, it would be a total of $224,736. Now I would have probably received some scholarships to go there, but with tuition and fees being so expensive, I probably would have had to take out some loans as well. So for $224,736, I would have received a graphic design degree making about $43,000 a year. In my mind I would have to give up my whole salary for a little over 5 years just to pay for the education that I received to obtain that salary and career (not including loan interest and fees and the taxes that are taken out of your salary). To me it did not seem like the best decision, so I opted to try other routes.

People steer other people in the wrong direction all the time. Luckily, I did my due-diligence; however, other people are not as lucky. I spoke to one person who was about to graduate college and asked her about her plans for after graduation. She told me that she will be going back to school to do pre-requisites for medical school. She continued on to say that she always knew that she wanted to be a doctor and go to medical school, but her Uncle (who is a doctor) told her to go to college to pursue her interests (which were women's studies and sociology) first. That way her application will look stronger when she applies to medical school because she will look like a well rounded student.

 That advice sounds good, but now she has already completed 4 years of college and will have to go back for another at least 2 years (or however long it takes her to complete the pre-requisites) before being able to apply to medical school. Instead of being able to apply to medical school and having a chance in 4 years, she will be applying to medical school after 6 years of college to see if she has that same chance. Meanwhile, she is acquiring more debt. Two extra years of school could mean an extra $20,000 of debt or more depending on what school you go to--- not including the debt that you already have from the first 4 years. And we have not even discussed or thought about the amount of debt that she will obtain from medical school which can easily adds up to over six figures. I hope her Uncle is paying for her schooling. If not, he has just steered her into a deep, deep downward spiraling hole of debt that will be difficult for even a doctor to dig herself out of.

What she should have done was majored in a subject like Biology or Chemistry or Physics (which would give her all of the pre-requisites necessary to

24

apply to medical school) and minored in women's studies or sociology (if she wanted to look well-rounded). That way she would have been able to apply to medical school and be on her way to becoming a doctor instead of still being in school doing pre-requisites. That would have been making the most out of her finances and time in college.

Friends and family are not the only ones that are misinformed. Guidance counselors and college advisors can lead you down the wrong path as well. (*Guidance counselors and college advisors mean well, don't get me wrong, sometimes they are misinformed or do not have all of the information necessary to steer you down the correct path. A lot of guidance counselors and college advisors are really helpful and really want to see you do your best.)

My high school guidance counselor encouraged me to apply to some of the more expensive and well known colleges, but financially I knew that was not the right way for me. I had a limited amount of money to spend on college applications (since I wanted to pay for all of my college application fees myself) and had to think logically about schools.

At that time I did not realize that is what I was doing but as soon as I got my first acceptance letter and saw the difference between the scholarships that I was awarded and the cost of attending the college, I understood that there was more to college than just picking any college or the most known college or the college that all of my friends were going to go to. I had to think of how I would pay for it. The school that you choose to attend can make the difference between you having to come up with $5,000 a year versus $50,000 or more a year so choose wisely.

I can also recall another time when one of my advisors sent me down the wrong path--- this time it was my college advisor. I visited my college advisor so that I could sign up for a class that I thought that I needed. I was planning on transferring to another school at the time so I made a list of all of the classes that I would need to take that semester that would transfer over to my new school. I printed this list directly off of the website. However, I started running out of ink in my printer and my paper had the course number but did not print out the course name so I just wrote it in quickly.

When my college advisor looked over my schedule before the final submission, she told me that I did not need that class and needed a different one for my graduation requirement based solely on the course name that I wrote down not matching up to the course number that was printed out. Listening to my advisor since I figured she knows best, she was the expert after all, I signed up for the class that she suggested. At the end of the semester, I found out that I was right with the class that I wrote down first and the college advisor had me take the wrong class. Taking that one wrong class could have cost

26

me $1,000. Also, It could have pushed back my graduation if that was my last semester in college, but I still had another semester left before I transferred to another school so luckily I was able to use that class as a general education requirement and took the right class the following semester--- the one that I signed up for first.

Please do not misinterpret what I am saying. People like friends, family members, guidance counselors, college advisors, admission officers, and financial aid officers have all of the best intensions in the world for you and your child. But, they can lead you on a path which may not always be the best path for your child. People advising you are most likely not taking the cost of college into much consideration; like my first example that I shared about my co-worker suggesting that I attend his Alma Mater, Boston University. In the end you and your child are paying for the college costs and acquiring the debt that it costs to go to the college--- not the other people that are advising you--- so it is your duty to figure out the best path for your individual circumstance.

Chapter 3

The FAFSA Facts

The FAFSA stands for Free Application for Federal Student Aid…

Wait! Don't skip this chapter just yet. A lot of people might be thinking, it is pointless for me to fill out the FAFSA because I make a good salary and will not be able to qualify for anything except loans. Well, that is not true, just keep reading.

The FAFSA is a form provided by the federal government that provides over $150 billion in grants, loans, and work-study funds each year. This will give you access to the largest source of financial aid for college. The FAFSA provides need-based (based on income of parent(s) and student) and merit-based (based on academic accomplishments) scholarships. File the FAFSA as soon as possible each year so that you won't miss any of the filing deadlines and to maximize your chance of getting the most money from your state, school, and from private scholarships. (There are some first-come first-serve grants and scholarships that are provided when you fill out the FAFSA so you always want to submit it early.) If you have any other questions about the FAFSA or want to file online, go to fafsa.ed.gov.

How Does the FAFSA Work?

The FAFSA form requests information on the parents' and student's income(s), savings accounts and other assets to assess financial need.

The Pros

The application is free.

Even if you think you won't qualify, fill it out anyways.

Most states, colleges, and universities use this to award other types of institutional grants and financial aid. This means that many colleges (and even private financial aid providers) use the FAFSA to award their own personal financial aid to you as well.

It is an excellent source for students with parents that have a lower income (less than $60,000 per year), low assets, and good academic grades.

When you file the FAFSA you are automatically applying for the Pell Grant and others.

The Cons

If the parents have a higher income (over $60,000) and assets, more financial aid will be awarded in the form of loans as compared to grants. (So it helps the lower- income students more, but remember other scholarships that you apply for or ones that you don't apply for and want to give you merit scholarships might require a FAFSA form to be filled out or will pull from this pool of applicants to award the scholarship to.)

If your child works while in college and makes over the amount required to file a tax return, the child's income can decrease the amount of financial aid that he will qualify for the following year.

The form is filled out each year so depending on changes in income and assets, the amount of aid awarded can vary each year.

For the Parents that Make Too Much

A lot of people think if you make over $50,000 or $60,000 a year, you will not be able to get any need-based financial aid. That is further from the truth. There are tricks that COLLEGE PLANNERS (not your accountant or your financial advisor) know that can help you receive need-based financial

32

aid. I would suggest that you consult with a COLLEGE PLANNER (once again NOT your accountant or your financial planner--- they just do not know the same tricks and tips that college planners know) so they can help you come up with a strategy to "move things around" and possibly help you get some need-based scholarships and grants from the FAFSA.

For example, one way some parents that make six-figures have been qualifying for need-based financial aid is by choosing a college that uses the 568 formula. With colleges that accept this formula, you are allowed to take all of the money that is sitting in your bank account (which would disqualify you for need-based financial aid because colleges and the FAFSA view money sitting in your bank account as money that is available for you to use to fund a college education) and pay down or pay off your home mortgage. By moving the money from your savings or checking account and into your mortgage, you will be able to qualify for some need-based financial aid. Whereas, leaving the money sitting in the account would only qualify you for loans.

Disclaimer: Always consult with a college planner before doing this. Every circumstance is different

One thing to remember is the financial aid forms are always based on the previous year, just like your tax returns. You really should consult with a college

33

planner early on so that you can plan when you will need to move around your assets. For instance, if you take all of your money out of your bank account in January 2013, it will not be taken into consideration for your child's financial aid award letter for the 2013-2014 school year because the 2013-2014 financial aid award letter is based on your income and assets from 2012.

If you need help finding a college planner to help you prepare for the FAFSA, go to **www.debtfreecollegegrad.com/contact** and send me an email.

The FAFSA can be a great tool. Utilize it. If you do not use it, you may lose out. If you use it and get nothing, you did not waste anything and are in the same position that you were before since it is a free application.

Chapter 4

Grants vs. Loans and Work- Study

In chapter 3, we discussed how the FAFSA provides over $150 billion each year in grants, loans, and work-study funds. When you fill out the form and receive your award package, you will see grants, loans, and sometimes work-study opportunities listed. What is the difference between the three? When I first looked at the financial aid paper, I was very confused on the difference so I am going to break it down for you.

Grants

One of the categories that you will see on the FAFSA is grants. Grants are essentially free money. This money does not have to be paid back and is given based on need-based or merit-based. The main grant given on the FAFSA is the *Pell Grant*.

I would ALWAYS accept this type of financial aid. Make sure that you check all boxes correctly so that you can accept this award. Speaking from experience, if you cannot check a box online, call and ask what you should do to make sure that you can accept this grant. I received a grant one time. I went online to accept the grants and there was one grant that would not let me check the box next to it. I figured it was an automatic grant so I did nothing. BIG MISTAKE. I ended up losing that $4,000 grant. When I called after the semester started to inquire about that grant, they said that since I did not accept it, they took it back. I guess I was supposed to mail in the form too to ensure that I accepted all the grants that were listed. I surely learned my lesson. After that, I started really paying attention and making sure that I checked the correct boxes. Any box that I was unable to check, I called to make sure AND mailed in a copy as well.

Loans

Another category that will be on the FAFSA financial aid award letter is loans. Loans have to be paid back. This is money that you are borrowing. When being awarded financial aid through the FAFSA form, you will see two main types of loans: the Stafford Loan (which can be broken down to unsubsidized and subsidized) and Perkins Loan.

Unsubsidized Stafford Loan: This is a loan where interest is accrued while the student is enrolled in school. (This means the student is getting charged interest on the loan while still in school.) The payments on the interest and the loan are deferred until after graduation. It has a fixed interest rate of 6.8%. This loan is available to all students.

Subsidized Stafford Loan: This is a loan where interest is NOT accrued on the loan while your child is in school or during the deferment period. The federal government will pay the interest during these times for the loan while the student is enrolled in college. The interest rate is fixed at about 3.5%. This is available to students based on financial need.

Perkins Loan: With this loan, interest does not start accruing until your child graduates. It is dependent on financial need based on the FAFSA and it has a fixed interest rate of 5%.

Remember my mother's advice to me? Stay away from loans. After that advice, I always stayed away from loans. Without you really knowing or paying attention, loans can quickly add up and put you on a downward spiral towards financial distress. Not only do loans quickly add up before graduation, but they also exponentially increase AFTER graduation due to interest and fees.

Work-Study

The last category that you will see on the FAFSA is work-study. To qualify for work-study, you also have to demonstrate financial need. Unlike the money that your child will earn from a part-time job, the work-study money that your child earns will not count against her when she applies for financial aid through the FAFSA for the next year. The Federal Work-Study Program guarantees your child a part-time job. The money for this part-time job will go towards tuition and other expenses.

I had a few friends that chose to do work-study. They all had very good things to say about it. They told me that the work was easy and they had a good amount of time to study for their classes while on the job. They also informed me that their hourly wage was a lot better than the standard minimum wage jobs that college students typically apply for. Instead of flipping burgers or working in a store at the mall for minimum wage, they were able to have a job which was on campus where they had the opportunity to study on the job. This means they did not have to worry about the cost to commute to work either.

***Disclaimer: Everyone's work-study experience will not be the same. Depending on the position that the work-study program gives you, you might not have as much free time while working to study or you might not make as much as another person doing work-study. You should look into the work-study programs and, if possible, ask the school for a few options before committing to one work-study job.

So to graduate with little to no debt, your child should aim to get more grants, and not loans. If your child does not qualify for a lot of grants through the

FAFSA, he should look for some scholarship opportunities.

Chapter 5

My #1 Tip for Getting EASY Scholarship Money

There is an abundance of scholarship opportunities for college students. You can get scholarships based on your GPA, SAT scores, community service performed and extra-curricular activities that your child is involved in. (No, you do NOT have to have the highest GPA or SAT scores to win some scholarships either.) However, a lot of students do not like to take the time to search for and apply to all of these scholarships.

My #1 tip for getting easy scholarship money does not require your child to submit a lot of essays to scholarship websites. All your child has to do is find schools that she is in the top 10 percent (or even 33 percent)--- or what guidance counselors call the "safety schools"--- and apply. This will be your child's *easiest way and best chance to obtain a full-ride scholarship*. When your student is in the top 10 percent, he will stand out from the crowd and qualify for merit scholarships at that college automatically.

Many schools offer automatic scholarships to students with certain GPAs and SAT scores to students that get accepted to the school. Also, colleges typically tend to give the most merit aid to their best students. (This principle also applies if your child is good at athletics or the program of study that he wants to get into.)

Just remember, each college is different. The GPA and SAT score requirements for one school might be higher or lower than another one. So with one school, your child may not be in the top 10 or 33 percent, but can be at a different college.

I noticed this tip when I was applying to colleges and received my financial aid award letter. I applied to 3 schools--- Towson University, University of Maryland Baltimore County, and some other private college. The private college letter came first. I opened it with anxious anticipation. The first thing I read was I was awarded around $20,000 in grants and scholarships for the college. I was too overjoyed as I ran around my room and screamed at the top of my lungs that I was accepted and had a lot of money for college. That was, until I took a second look. Yes, the private college awarded me $20,000 for the whole year in grants; however, it cost $40,000 for the year just to attend the school. They kindly listed some loans that I could take out at the bottom of the paper. After seeing how much the school cost, I quickly tossed that paper aside.

Next up was the financial aid award letter for University of Maryland Baltimore County. By the time this letter came in, I was already an expert at financial aid award reviewing from my first occurrence. Since the University of Maryland Baltimore County was a public college, the tuition and fees were a lot less than the private college. This college only cost around $20,000 for the year and they were nice enough to award me with $13,000 in grants and scholarships. Although that was a nice gesture, in my mind, I still had to come up with $7,000 each year or $3,500 each semester. I tossed this letter to the "maybe" pile.

Up last was Towson University's award letter. Hesitantly, I opened it expecting them to have something about a loan or extra money that I would have to pay each semester. I was no longer going to get my hopes up. To my surprise, Towson University awarded me full tuition. The school cost about the same amount to attend as the University of Maryland Baltimore County did. But, Towson University generously gave me a long list of scholarships and grants that totaled to the same amount of the cost of attendance at the college. Immediately I decided this would be the college that I would attend. I would not have to take out any loans or worry about how I would pay the tuition each semester. Towson University was in the "no brainer/ you better accept this award" pile.

When it comes down to actually choosing a college, you need to consider the financial aid award package. The students do not really know what it is like to attend a particular college until after they get there so how are they supposed to know that it is their "dream school" beforehand? Also, keep in mind that most students usually transfer to a different college at some point during their 4 year (or 6 year) college career. Although Towson University gave me a full-ride, I still had to switch to a different college after my first semester because I decided to change my major to one that Towson University did not offer. A lot of my friends ended up changing colleges as well. Some could not afford the cost of their college anymore while others did not like the college as much as they thought they were going to.

From these experiences, I learned that you should apply to schools where your child is at the top of the class. Your child can still apply to the schools that she wants, but also keep in mind the "safety schools." The "safety" schools will award the best financial aid packages because they really want your child to represent their school and to attend. Always remember, the best financial aid award packages will equal the best situation for your wallet, bank account, retirement fund, and child's future.

Chapter 6

Apply for Scholarships

Before I started college, I was on my way to being part of the student loan statistic that we mentioned in the first chapter. I did not think about the costs associated with going to college when I applied to the colleges. All I knew was that everyone wanted me to go to college and I was going--- I didn't really have an option. However, everything changed when my cousin came to visit.

My cousin graduated college one semester before I graduated high school. She came over the summer before I went to college seeming discouraged and frustrated because she graduated over 6 months ago and still could not find a job in her chosen major. To make matters worse, her student loan payments were about to kick in. (Yes, even if you cannot find a job after you graduate college, you are still responsible for paying back your student loans.) Then my cousin looked up at me and said the most important, life changing thing that anyone has ever told me about college.

She said, "You really need to consider college costs when you go to college." This solidified what I had a slight hint about from chapter 2--- that the more a college costs to attend, the more money you would need to pay for it--- but this interpretation did not cover everything that she meant. I took her advice into deep consideration, but I did not understand it fully until I lost that $4,000 scholarship. It was then that I realized that she was not just talking about tuition, room and board. My cousin was also talking about extra expenses like scholarships that do not go through until after the semester begins or scholarships that get taken back or books, school supplies, transportation, and other miscellaneous expenses. Even if a school gives you a full-ride, unless you are getting a stipend as well, you will still need more money for college.

When I lost that $4,000 scholarship, I had to do something quick so I started looking into scholarships. Applying for scholarships and receiving the scholarships that I applied for is what made the difference between me having to pay for college and me receiving refund checks each semester. Who wants to pay for school when you can get paid to go to school?

I know by now some of you might be thinking, "I don't have a high GPA so I will not be able to qualify or I will not win the scholarship. There are so many people that are better academically than I am." Despite popular belief, you do not have to have the highest GPA or SAT scores. Some scholarships do not have a GPA requirement while others might only require you to have at least a 2.5 GPA. Once you meet that minimum GPA requirement, GPA is no longer a deciding factor. The judges will start to look at your scholarship application as a whole and not just focus on your GPA.

Also, there are literally scholarships for everyone! Academic scholarships, or scholarships that require a high GPA, are only one type of scholarship. There are athletic scholarships, scholarships for women, scholarships for people interested in religion, scholarships for dancers and artists, scholarships for people with disabilities, and an abundance of others. In the next chapter, I have listed some different types of scholarships just so you can see how many types of scholarships are available.

Now that the GPA myth is out of the way, let's tackle another scholarship myth.

Some others are probably thinking, "Don't you have to apply and receive over 100 scholarships in order to cover your college costs? That seems like a lot of work, time, and scholarship applications that I would have to fill out and win." That is not true either. I used my #1 tip for getting easy scholarship money (from the previous chapter) in conjunction with applying for scholarships so I did not have to apply for 100 scholarships. I did not even have to apply for 50 scholarships. You only have to apply and win as many scholarships as it costs to attend the school.

Say for instance, if I went to the University of Maryland Baltimore County. Remember, they gave me $13,000 in automatic grants, but the school costs $20,000 to attend. That is $7,000 that I would need to get from winning scholarships just to cover the tuition and room and board. $7,000 seems like a lot of money, but a lot of scholarships are $500 or more. Say the majority of the scholarships are $1,000 on average. That means if each scholarship that you win is $1,000 you would only need to win 7 scholarships to get the money necessary to attend college. Any other scholarships that you won after the first 7 would just be money in the bank and could go to your miscellaneous expenses.

Where to Find Scholarships

By now you are probably getting excited and wondering where can you find these scholarships so you can start applying right now.

There are many books and websites that your child can use to find scholarships to apply to. I tried to apply for scholarships on FastWeb.com with no luck. I did not hear anything. I could not even get a call back. I know there are a lot of people in this same boat. It's VERY discouraging. I wanted to just give up on scholarship searching altogether. I learned that FastWeb.com is a well-known site. Although they have millions of scholarships that they list, there are also millions of people from all over the world utilizing that database so there is a lot of competition for the same scholarships. I found that the scholarships that I applied to that I heard back and received the scholarship award from were local scholarships, state scholarships, and scholarships that a financial aid advisor or someone else told me about. These scholarships typically have less people applying for them than the Gates Millennium Scholar Program or the Coca-Cola

Scholarship so there will be less competition. Scholarships that have less people competing for the winnings will give you a greater chance of winning the scholarship.

I once had someone tell me about a scholarship when I was working a summer job. I was a teller at a bank and called the next customer to come up. The next customer happened to be an older couple who wanted to make a simple deposit into their account. I gave the customers good customer service, like how corporate trained us, and at the end of the couple's transaction she asked her husband to hand her a card. She then handed the card to me and said, "I think you might be a good candidate for our scholarship fund." I went home to apply immediately, but that year's scholarship deadline had just passed. I held onto that scholarship information until the next year and ended up winning the $2,000 scholarship. I applied again the following year, which happened to be my last year of college, and won again!

I know not everyone has people just handing them information on scholarship applications. I really just had that one scholarship application literally handed to me. For other scholarships, I had to do more research to find them.

I found out about another scholarship that I ended up winning through conversation. I ran into a friend that I went to high school with one day. We started talking about how college was going and scholarships were mentioned. She told me that she applied to the Senator and Delegate scholarship for our state and won. I looked up those state scholarships that she told me about and applied and won as well.

Often, you can ask your friends what scholarships they have won for some ideas on where to apply. I would also suggest that you ask your high school guidance counselor what scholarships students at your high school have won in previous years and what scholarship applications they have in the office. They might be able to provide you with a list of scholarships that you can look into to see if you are eligible.

If you have exhausted all of the scholarships that your high school or college has and that your friends have recommended, try calling or visiting neighboring high schools and colleges in your area or even throughout your state to ask what scholarships they have. Some schools receive different scholarships than other schools but you may still be able to apply. The scholarship that I mentioned earlier that was handed to me when I was working at a bank was not a scholarship that the guidance counselors at my high school had. The scholarship committee only went to a few high schools that were closer to where they lived to advertise the scholarship fund even though the scholarship application did not have any restrictions on where you lived.

Another way that you can find even more local and community scholarships that are available to you is to do a Google search of the scholarships in your area. All you have to do is type in your Google search bar your city or the region that you reside in plus the words "community foundation" after. For example, you could type in "Los Angeles community foundation" or "Washington community foundation."

Scholarships from local, community resources are less advertised or are only available to students in a particular area, thus, there is less competition for the scholarships. Since there is less competition, these scholarships will have a better probability of you winning them.

For more help on finding scholarships that you can win, go to **www.debtfreecollegegrad.com**

Along with suggesting that you apply for scholarships in your community, I have three main tips that helped me when I was applying for scholarships that I would like to share with you.

1. The first thing is to make sure that you are eligible for the scholarship. You do not want to fill out a scholarship and you do not meet the criteria to apply. This will just waste your child's time. For example, a scholarship for piano players might require

that you write a song that you will have to play on the piano. Do not apply if you do not know how to play the piano. Another example is if the scholarship requires you to have a 3.0 GPA. If you do not have a 3.0 or higher, you typically should not apply. *There is an exception to this rule. One of my friends did not have the minimum GPA required for an aviation scholarship so he did not apply. Later, he found out that no one applied to get that scholarship for that year so if he would have applied, they would have made an exception for him and he most likely would have received the scholarship money.

2. Second, make sure that your child meets the deadlines provided. A lot of scholarships have early deadlines for submission. I missed the deadline for that one scholarship that I just mentioned, but remembered to apply earlier the following year and ended up receiving that scholarship for the next two years. Scholarship committees are typically very strict about having applications in or postmarked by the deadline. If your application is not there by the deadline, you will most likely be disqualified. A lot of judges will not even look at your application no matter how "perfect" you are for the scholarship fund if it is not received by the deadline. As a personal rule, I always like to turn my

scholarship package in as early as possible. Sometimes the mail can get to the scholarship committee slower than you thought or if you are submitting your application online, it could get lost in "cyber space." Another thing that happens is when you go to submit online on the due date, you might get an error message when trying to submit or the website might be not working correctly. By always submitting my application early, I was not worried if the judges received my application or not on time. I knew they would get it earlier rather than later.

3. Third, make sure that you follow the scholarship application directions carefully. You must read all of the scholarship application directions before you start the application and make sure that you are following all of the directions precisely. These directions will let you know everything that you need to include in your application and everything that the judges are looking at to see if you are a good candidate for their scholarship. If you do not include everything that the scholarship requires, like the essay or your transcripts, you will be automatically exempt from winning the scholarship. Also, some essays have a minimum or maximum word requirement. For example, if the essay asks you to write a 300-500 word essay, stay

within those parameters. Do not write an essay that is 501 words or one that is 297 words or even one that is 300 or 301 or 302 words. If the judges are counting the words in your essay, they might miscount or count fewer words than you may have counted. In order to prevent yourself from being disqualified, write at least ten more words than the minimum amount and ten fewer words than the maximum required amount of words. Using this rule, your desired essay that requires a word count between 300 to 500 words would be 310 to 490 words. Sometimes the deciding factor between you winning the scholarship and someone else is who followed directions the best.

Following these three steps will help your child find scholarships that he or she is more likely to obtain.

If you ever need any help with finding scholarships or filling out award winning scholarship applications, visit **www.debtfreecollegegrad.com**

Chapter 7

List of Scholarships

As promised, here is a list of different types of scholarships.

Acting Scholarships (for those who want to be an actor or actress)

- Screen Actors Guild John L. Dales Scholarship Fund
  - www.sagfoundation.org/programs/scholarships

- Irene Ryan Acting Scholarships
  - www.kennedy-center.org/education/actf/actfira.html

- NYCDA (New York conservatory for Dramatic Arts' School of Film and Television) Scholarships
  - www.sft.edu/scholarships/nycda-scholarships.html

Atheist Scholarship (for those who don't believe in God)

- Atheists for Human Rights Award
  - www.atheistsforhumanrights.org
  - www.pfundonline.org/scholarship-win.html

Aviation Scholarships (for those who are interested in airplanes)

- Santa Rosa Ninety Nines Aviation Scholarship
    - www.ninety-nines.org/index.cfm/other_scholarships.htm

- Archie C. Towle Aviation Scholarship
    - www.cfoncw.org/media/scholarships/Towle,%20Archie%20C.doc

- League of World War I Aviation Historians' Mike Carr Student Paper Award
    - www.ofas.uci.edu/content/outsidescholarships.aspx?nav=0&id=1157

- Leroy W. Homer Jr. Scholarship
    - www.leroywhomerjr.org/scholarships

- GRCF Joshua Esch Mitchell Aviation Scholarship
    - www.grfoundation.org/scholarshipslist

Bible Scholarships (for those who study the Bible)

- Italian Catholic Federation Scholarships
  - www.icf.org

- John W. McDevitt (Fourth Degree) Scholarships
  - www.kofc.org/un/en/scholarships/mc devitt.html

- Tessie Eerligh Scharing Memorial Scholarship
  - www.faithandeducation.org/

Cancer Scholarships (for people who are cancer survivors)

- Cancer for College
  - www.cancerforcollege.org

- Cancer Survivors' Fund
  - www.cancersurvivorsfund.org

- Youth Cancer Survivor College Scholarship
  - www.cancersurvivorsfund.org
  - www.stmfoundation.org/ortherschola rships.html
  - www.cancer.org/myacs/midwest/you thscholarship

- Miles of Hope Breast Cancer Foundation Scholarship
  - Milesofhope.org/funds

Scholarships for Single Mothers

- Jeannette Rankin Foundation Scholarships
  - www.rankinfoundation.org

- Patsy Takemoto Mink Foundation Scholarship
  - www.patsyminkfoundation.org

- Arizona Business & Professional Women's Foundation Scholarships
  - www.arizonabpwfoundation.com/scholarships.html

- Women's Opportunity Award (Washington, DC)
  - www.soroptimist.org/awards/awards.html

- Arkansas Single Parent Scholarship Fund
  - www.aspsf.org

- Women's Opportunity Award
  - www.soroptimist.org

Scholarships for Community Service

- Alliant Energy Community Service Scholarship
  - www.alliantenergy.com/communityinvolvement

- The Disneyland Resort Scholarship Program
  - Publicaffairs.disneyland.comdisneyland-resort-scholarship-program-requirements

- Prudential Spirit of Community Awards
  - Spirit.prudential.com

- Samuel Huntington Public Service Award
  - www.nationalgridus.com/huntington.asp

Dance Scholarships

- Furman University Art Scholarships
  - www2.furman.edu/academics/art

- The George Snow Scholarship Fund
  - www.scholarship.org

Scholarships for People with Disabilities

- Scholarship for People with Disabilities
  - www.disabled-world.com/disability/education/scholarships

- 180 Medical Scholarship Program
  - www.180medical.com/scholarships

- JCS Newhoff Scholarship for a Jewish Student with a Diagnosed Learning Disability
  - www.jcsbaltimore.org

- Through the Looking Glass Scholarships for Students with Parents with Disabilities
  - www.lookingglass.org

Essay Writing Scholarships

- Washington State Association for Justice American Justice Essay Scholarship
  - www.washingtonjustice.org

- Growing Up Asian in America Art & Essay Contest
  - www.asianpacificfund.org

- ALBA George Watt Memorial Essay Contest
    - www.alba-valb.org/participate/essay-contest

- FRA Americanism Essay Contest
    - www.fra.org/Content/fra/AboutFRA/EssayContest

- IAPMO Scholarship Essay Contest
    - www.iapmo.org/pages/essaycontest.aspx

First Generation College Student Scholarships
(Or simply be the first one in your family to attend college)

- Carol A. Hurley Memorial Scholarship
    - www.vsac.org

- TELACU David C. Lizarraga Fellowship
    - Telacu.com/site/en/home/education/applications.html

- TELACU Scholarship Program
    - Telacu.com

- College Assistance Migrant Program
    - www2.ed.gov/programs/camp
    - www.csusm.edu/camp

- www.migrantstudents.org/campappli cants.html

- Catawba College's First Family Scholarships
  - www.catawba.edu

- Diamonds in the Rough Ministry International Scholarship
  - Diamondsntherough.org/scholarship. html

- Human Capital Scholarship
  - www.ofas.uci.edu/content/outsidesch olarships.aspx
  - www.asianpacificfund.org/informati on-for-student-applicants
  - www.rwjf.org/en/about- rwjf/program-areas/human- capital.html

- I'm First Scholarship
  - www.imfirst.org/scholarship

International Student/ Study Abroad Scholarships

- AWS International Scholarship Program
  - www.aws.org/w/a/foundation/intl_sc holarships.html

- American Association of University Women International Fellowships
  - www.aauw.org/what-we-do/educational-funding-and-awards

- NSCS Academy Abroad Scholarship
  - www.nscs.org/scholarships

- SIT Study Abroad HBCU Scholarships
  - www.sit.edu/studyabroad/scholarshi ps.htm

Legacy Scholarships

- ENF Legacy Awards for the Children of Elks
  - www.elks.org/enf/scholars/legacy.cf m

- The GCSAA Legacy Awards
  - www.gcsaa.org

- Augustana College Alumni Legacy Award
    - www.augie.edu

- VCSU Aluni Upper-Level Scholarships
    - www.vcsu.edu

Military Scholarships (you can qualify for some if your parents are in the military as well)

- Fisher House Foundation Scholarships for Military Children
    - www.fisherhouse.org/programs
    - www.militaryscholar.org

- Army Staff Sgt. Special Agent Richard S. Eaton Jr. Scholarship
    - Lintcenter.org/scholarships.htm

Minority Scholarships

- African American Scholarships
    - Blackstudents.blacknews.com
    - www.littleafrica.com/scholarship

- Hispanic Scholarships
  - www.hsf.net
  - www.latinocollegedollars.org

- Native American Scholarships
  - www.niea.org/scholarships
  - www.catchingthedream.org/scholarship.htm
  - indiancountrytodaymedianetwork.com/department/scholarships

Religious Scholarships

- Baptist Scholarships
  - www.baylor.edu

- Buddhist Scholarships
  - www.uwest.edu
  - www.maitripa.org

- Catholic Scholarships
  - www.kofc.org/en/scholarships/index.html
  - www.catholic.org/college/scholarships.php

- Christian Scholarships
  - www.yclscholarship.org
  - www.lcu.edu

- Episcopalian Scholarships
  - www.episcopalchurch.org/scholarships
  - stpaulsec.org
  - www.dioms.org/scholarship/index.html

- Hindu Scholarships
  - www.thehindu.com
  - hinduscholarship.org

- Jewish Scholarships
  - www.jewishfed.org/scholarships
  - www.jewishcamp.org

- Lutheran Scholarships
  - www.valpo.edu
  - www.wlc.edu/scholarships
  - www.womenoftheelca.org/scholarships-pages-57.php

- Methodist Scholarships
  - www.umhef.org
  - www.gbhem.org

- Muslim Scholarships
  - www.isna.net/scholarships.html
  - islanicscholarshipfund.org
  - muslimscholarship.org

- Pagan/ Wiccan Scholarships
  - www.carolinaspiritquest.org

- Presbyterian Scholarships
  - www.presbyterianmission.org

Poetry Scholarships

- Ruth Lilly Poetry Fellowships
  - www.poetryfoundation.org

- Poetry Out Loud Scholarship Contest
  - www.poetryoutloud.org

Scholarships for Men

- The Mervyn Sluizer, Jr. Scholarship
  - www.philafound.org
  - www.bccbsa.org

- Balanced Man Scholarship
    - www.sigep.org
    - www.gwsigeps.com/balanced-man-scholarship
    - www.sigeptnkappa.org/balanced-man-scholarship

- Tex Schramm Freshman Scholarship
    - www.utphipsi.com
    - utphipsi.chaptercore.com/forms/165

- Darryl Jahn Memorial Scholarship
    - Epsilon.betasigmapsi.org

- Mike Hylton and Ron Niederman Scholarship
    - www.hemophiliafed.org

Science and Technology Scholarships

- Jim and Anna Hyonjoo Lint Scholarship
    - www.lintcenter.org

- Minnesota Space Grant Consortium
    - www.aem.umn.edu/msgc

- Medical and Health Professions Scholarship
  - www.med.navy.mil
  - www.goarmy.com/amedd/education/hpsp.html
  - www.ttuhsc.edu/admissions/army_hpsp.aspx

Weird and Unusual Scholarships

- Tall Clubs International Student Scholarships
  - Tall.org/tci-acts-scholarships-2

- National Potato Council Scholarship
  - Nationalpotatocouncil.org/events-and-programs/scholarship-program

- Little People of America Scholarships
  - www.lpaonline.org/scholarships-and-grants

- Annual Create-A-Greeting-Card Scholarship Contest
  - www.gallerycollection.com/greeting-cards-scholarship.htm

- Asparagus Club Scholarship
  - www.braf.org/assets/docs/scholarshi
    ps/AsparagusScholarship.pdf
  - www.nationalgrocers.org

- Chick and Sophie Major Memorial Duck
  Calling Contest
  - www.stuttgartarkansas.org/duck-
    festival/scholarship_contest.aspx

- Duck Brand Stuck at Prom Scholarship
  Contest
  - www.duckbrand.com/index.php/pro
    motions/stuck-at-prom

- International Dairy-Deli-Bakery Assn.
  Scholarship
  - www.iddba.org/scholarships.aspx

- Ludo Frevel Crystallography Scholarship
  Award
  - www.icdd.com

- Minnesota Soybean Ambassador Program
  - www.mnsoybean.org/

- American Fire Sprinkler Association
  Scholarship Program
  - www.afsascholarship.org

- Beef Industry Scholarship
  - www.nationalcattlemensfoundation.org

- The Collegiate Inventors Competition
  - Collegiateinventors.org

- Chick Evans Caddie Scholarship
  - www.wgaesf.org

These are not even half of the scholarships that are available for you to apply to! More scholarships and help with filling out scholarship applications can be found on **www.debtfreecollegegrad.com**. Now you can see just how plentiful scholarships are. You do not have to have the highest GPA or SAT scores. Your parents do not have to have a low income either. There is a scholarship literally for everything that you can think of and there are scholarships out there that are specifically just for you.

Chapter 8

Final Remarks

I was able to graduate college debt- free with money in the bank and you can too! Despite popular belief, I did not have the highest GPA or SAT scores and my parents were in the middle class. Also, graduating college debt-free with money in the bank was not as difficult as I thought it would be. Sure, I made some mistakes along the way and it would have been way easier and less time consuming if I had someone holding my hand along the way to show me the ropes, but it still got done. By following these 5 simple steps, you can be on your way to graduating college debt-free too:

1. Choosing an affordable college
2. Applying to schools where you are in the top 10%
3. Doing your own due-diligence when making college decisions
4. Filling out the FAFSA
5. Applying for other outside scholarships

This is just the beginning of the things that you need to know to graduate college debt free. Now you understand the effects of acquiring school debt and how it adds up fast. I have shown you how people can steer your child in the wrong direction when it comes to college decisions, which also will increase college costs, and the facts behind the FAFSA. You have also learned the difference between grants, scholarships, and the Work-Study Program and the easiest way to get free scholarship money and hopefully a full-ride scholarship.

For more information on being a debt free college graduate and to access my step-by-step system for finding and winning scholarships for college, visit **www.debtfreecollegegrad.com**.

Chapter 9

Scholarship FAQs

What is a merit scholarship?

A merit scholarship is free money for college. It does not have to be paid back and it is NOT based on your parents' income (although some merit scholarships can have a financial need requirement as well). This scholarship is given based on the student's achievements in areas such as academic achievements (like your SAT scores or GPA), community service, hobbies, career goals, leadership skills, ethnicity, athletics, and many other areas.

There are two different types of merit scholarships:

1. Institutional merit scholarships and
2. Private merit scholarships.

What are institutional merit scholarships?

Institutional merit scholarships are given to the students by the college usually based on the student's academic achievements like their GPAs or SAT scores or even athletic abilities. These are automatic scholarships that the colleges will give to their top applicants to persuade them to attend their college instead of another college. (This means that you can only use it at that particular school that is giving you the institutional aid.) Remember, colleges want the best students to represent them so they will compete for you to attend through these institutional scholarships. You can be considered a top student at one college while only an average student at another--- it just all depends on the individual college's average student's statistics. Institutional merit scholarships are typically renewable (meaning you can use these scholarships for all 4 years of your undergraduate college career), but you have to follow the institution's rules for being able to renew the scholarship. These rules might include maintaining a specific GPA, for example a 3.2 or higher, and taking a minimum amount of credits each semester, like you have to take at least 12 credits each semester.

What are private merit scholarships?

Private merit scholarships can be used for any college that you decide to attend. They are usually offered by organizations, businesses, or individuals. They look for students with characteristics and goals that align with the values and goals of their organization. The student has to submit a scholarship application which will be reviewed by the scholarship judges and the judges will chose who will receive the scholarship funds. Each private scholarship has different rules and guidelines so make sure that you understand them. Private scholarships are the scholarships that you would focus on if your strengths are in areas besides academics. There are an abundance of private scholarships offered based on your hobbies, artistic talent, community service, leadership, etcetera that do not require you to list your GPA, SAT scores, or parent's income. The scholarship awards will vary from a few hundred dollars to thousands of dollars based on the scholarship that you are applying to. The deadlines for these scholarships are all year round--- it just depends on the scholarship that you are applying for.

Can I win merit scholarships even if my parents make a lot of money?

Yes. Most merit scholarships do not ask for you to disclose your parent's income or assets. Merit scholarships will be awarded to you based on your achievements, whether they are academically, athletically, artistically, through community service, interests or hobbies, or even unique things about you such as disabilities, your heritage, and memberships that you possess. Your parents can be millionaires and you will still be able to qualify for some merit scholarships.

I have a low GPA and/or low SAT scores. Will I still be able to qualify for scholarships?

Yes. A lot of private merit scholarships do not require you to include your GPA or SAT scores. There are scholarships that will only ask you to write an essay or put together a portfolio or use your creative skills in another way. Also, even if there is a GPA requirement, sometimes it is only a 2.5 or 3.0 minimum. Once you meet the minimum requirement for that specific scholarship, you are eligible to apply.

After graduating from college, do you have to pay back the money that you received from scholarships or grants?

No. Scholarships and grants are considered "free" money for college. You do NOT have to pay this money back after graduation. However, loans do have to be paid back after graduation. You might see both options on the FAFSA or financial aid award letters, but always remember that loans have to be paid back (with interest) and scholarships and grants do not have to be paid back.

Do you have to wait until your senior year of high school after you submitted your college applications before you can apply for scholarships?

No. There are scholarships that are available for high school, middle school, and even elementary students. For example, students that are in grades 6-8 can apply to the Christopher Columbus Community Service Award Scholarship. Since students are so young, the award will be in the form of a savings bond. Another example is the Doodle 4 Google scholarship where children in kindergarten through 12th grade can submit their own Google logo. There is another scholarship called the Jif Most Creative Peanut Butter Sandwich Contest which is open to children that are 6 to 12 years of age. I actually encourage students to start applying for scholarships as early as possible. Applying earlier for scholarships will help you obtain funding for college gradually over time instead of rushing and being stressed trying to fill out as many applications as you can in the few weeks or months before college begins.

When should I start preparing to apply for scholarships?

Ideally, it is best to start preparing to apply for scholarships the summer before you enter into high school. If you start looking at scholarships and their eligibility requirements that early, you will have a lot of time to sign up for community service experiences and extra-curricular activities that will spark your interest and also correspond with the scholarship opportunities that you are researching. Starting early when applying for scholarships will give you time to make sure that you can make yourself eligible for the scholarships that you are interested in. For instance, a scholarship might require you to have a 3.0 GPA when you only have a 2.8 GPA. Since you started researching scholarships early, you can work on increasing your GPA so you will be eligible to apply the following year. Or say if you needed 100 community service hours to be eligible but you only had 90 hours. Now you have the time to get the extra 10 hours that you will need to be eligible. Or if you needed to be a member of a particular group; since you started early you can now apply for membership to be in that group and will be eligible to apply for that scholarship.

Is it too late to apply for scholarships after the spring time of your senior year in high school?

No. Private scholarships will have deadlines that are all throughout the school year. You will just have to find and apply for those scholarships with deadlines that have not passed yet. There are a lot of scholarships with deadlines in the spring or fall, but there are also plenty of scholarships that have deadlines in the summer and winter months.

Where can I find scholarship opportunities?

Scholarship opportunities are literally everywhere. There are a lot of scholarship books that come out yearly that you can purchase or get from your library and there are a lot of scholarship databases like Fastweb and Scholarships.com that you can find scholarships. However, the best place that I have found scholarships were in my local community. Asking guidance counselors and financial aid officers about scholarships that they know or that students have won in the past were the scholarships that I received the best results from. Also, you can do a Google search for foundations in your local area which will show you some other scholarship opportunities. You can even do a Google search with your area and the word "scholarships" which will help you find some, but the best place to start is at your high school or college.

Are there scholarship opportunities available to college students?

Yes, college students are still eligible for scholarships. You will find these at the college that you attend through the financial aid office or you can ask your department chair or even some of your professors about scholarships in the field of study that you are interested in. If you want to venture out and find scholarships outside of your school, you can ask other colleges in your area for scholarships that they have received from private organizations. Just make sure that your age fits the eligibility requirement of the specific scholarship and you will be able to qualify.

Are there scholarship opportunities for graduate students? (This includes professional students like law, medicine, dental, etc)

Yes, graduate students should look into fellowships that their school provides. In addition, graduate students will want to search for scholarships based on their area of study and their interests. There is an abundance of scholarship opportunities for graduate students. Graduate students just have to know where to look and make sure that they fit the eligibility requirement of the specific scholarship.

I do not like writing essays. Can I still apply to scholarships?

Although a lot of scholarship applications require an essay component, not all of them do. Some scholarship applications will ask you to make a video, use your creativity skills, submit a portfolio of your work, write a poem, read a passage and take a quiz on it, or will require you to do something else. If you do not like to write essays, try to find scholarships that do not have an essay requirement.

Writing essays for scholarships are not as bad as you think. A lot of scholarships ask the same or similar essay questions so you do not always have to write a new essay for each scholarship application. If you do not like writing essays, gather a few applications that have a similar essay question and create one essay. Then slightly edit that one essay that you wrote to tailor it towards the other scholarship applications that require you to write a similar essay. Using one essay and customizing it for different scholarship applications saved me a lot of time and made applying for scholarships very easy.

How can I figure out which colleges will offer me the most institutional aid (automatic scholarships)?

The colleges where you are overqualified for will offer you the most institutional aid. These will be the schools that your guidance counselor will refer to as your "safety schools." You will have a higher GPA and/or SAT score than the school's average GPA and SAT scores that they report on their website for the average student. Remember, schools want students that they think will represent them well. If you are above the school's average standard, you will have a good chance of being a student that the school will want to attend and represent their school. Colleges will always compete for the "best students" by giving them more money in automatic scholarships or institutional aid.

How can I receive refund checks back from the college?

Get more money in scholarships than what it costs to attend the college.

Always check with the individual college. Each college may be different in regards to refund checks. However, I was able to receive refund checks back from the college by winning more money in scholarships than what it cost to attend the college. After the college's tuition and fees were paid, the college would send me a check for what was left over.

How can I graduate college debt-free?

Three things that I always tell people when they ask me how to graduate college debt-free is to:

1. Apply for colleges where you are their top student.
2. Make smart decisions when choosing a college.
3. Apply for outside private scholarships.

Applying for colleges where you are their top student will give you a lot of institutional aid (automatic scholarships) to start off with so you will not have to apply to hundreds of scholarships in order to afford the tuition.

Then you have to make smart decisions based on the cost of attending the college and how much the college is giving you each semester. One college can provide you with a lot of scholarship money to attend, but if it costs a lot of money to attend that college, you have to ask yourself if it will be affordable. For example, College A gives you $20,000 each year in institutional aid but it costs $40,000 to attend each year. With that college you will still have to come up with $20,000 each year to attend. College B gives you $10,000 each year in institutional aid but costs $20,000 per year to attend. With College B you will only have to come up with $10,000 extra each year to attend. Which would be the better choice financially? College B.

Last apply for private scholarships. Even if you get a full-ride scholarship, costs like books and living expenses might not be covered. Private scholarships should help supplement the difference between the institutional aid and the cost of attending the college so you won't have to pay to go to college.

These three things will help you graduate college debt-free.

ABOUT THE AUTHOR

 Shanice Miller, RDH, BS, author, scholarship specialist, and motivational speaker, avoided over $200,000 in student loans. Through winning an abundance of scholarships and her own due diligence, she graduated from college 100% debt-free. In 2011, she graduated from The University of Maryland Baltimore, College of Dental Surgery with a degree in dental hygiene. The entire cost of her college education and more was paid for through scholarship winnings. She even received refund checks back from the college due to receiving more scholarship money than what the school cost to attend. With that extra money, she was able to purchase her first home just two months after her graduation.

Known as "The Debt Free College Queen," Miller has advised many students and parents on college scholarships, majors, and careers. She is also the founder of debtfreecollegegrad.com, which is a leading online resource for teaching students how to graduate from college debt free.

Prior to college, Miller attended Charles Herbert Flowers High School in Springdale, Maryland, where she took part in their prestigious science and technology program. She also held prominent positions in the National English Honor Society and in the school yearbook and tutored numerous students. Among other awards and honors, she was awarded "Student of the Year" for all four consecutive years in her science and technology program.

Miller currently resides in Maryland and can be contacted via e-mail at **info@debtfreecollegegrad.com**. For more information, visit **www.debtfreecollegegrad.com**.

33635876R00062

Made in the USA
Charleston, SC
20 September 2014